THE GROSVENORS OF

The Dukes of Westminster and Their Forebears

by

Diana Newton and Jonathan Lumby

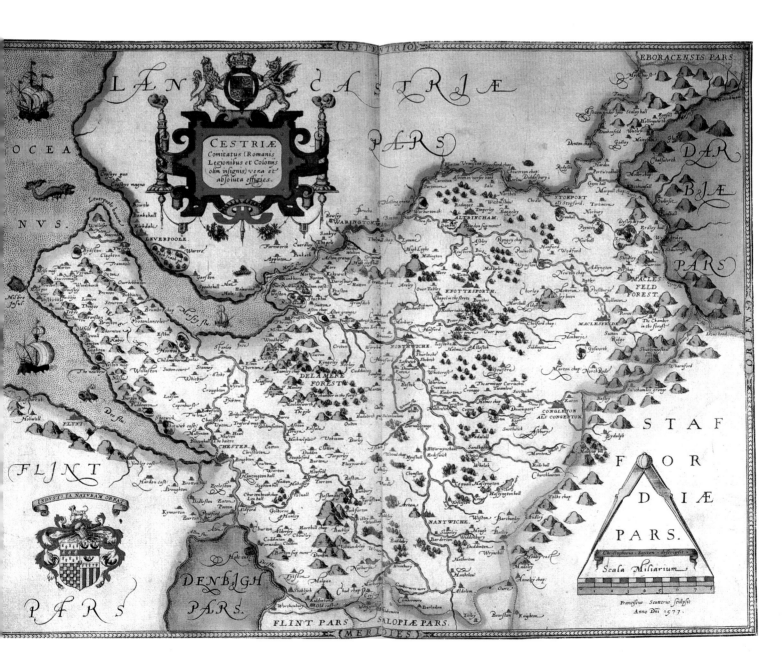

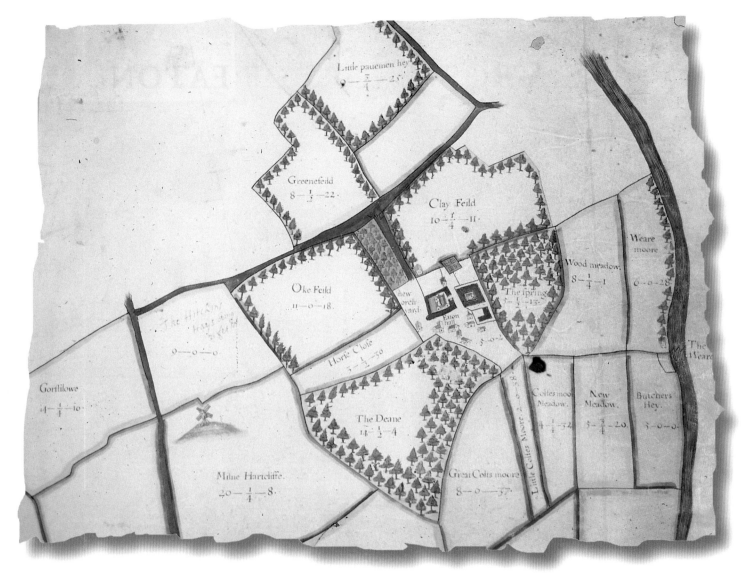

A seventeenth-century century map of the Eaton estate, showing the hall amidst enclosed farmland.

Text copyright © Diana Newton and Jonathan Lumby

Published in 2002 by
Jennet Publications,
The Rectory,
Church Road,
Eccleston,
Chester,
CH4 9HT
Tel: 01244 674703

ISBN 1-9543379-0-5

British Library Cataloguing-in-Publication data
A catalogue record for this book is available from the British Library

Typeset, designed and originated by
Carnegie Publishing Ltd, Lancaster, *www.wooof.net*
Printed and bound in the UK
by Cromwell Press, Trowbridge

Contents

Dr Diana Newton is a Research Fellow at the University of Teesside. Her *Papists, Protestants and Puritans 1559–1714* is published by Cambridge University Press (1998).

The Revd. Jonathan Lumby, author of *The Lancashire Witch Craze, 1612* (Carnegie, 1998) is Rector of Eccleston.

The authors gratefully acknowledge the help of:

Eileen Simpson, archivist to the Duke of Westminster;

David Cummings, who photographed documents;

Dr Sally Roxburgh, who helped prepare the text for publication;

His Grace the Duke of Westminster, for supporting this presentation of his family's history.

Sources of illustrations

Most illustrations are of pictures and documents in the Grosvenor Collections and are published by kind permission of His Grace the Duke of Westminster OBE TE DL and the Trustees of the Grosvenor Estate.

The following also allowed reproduction of pictures and documents:

Anne, Duchess of Westminster:
   G. Stubbs, *Mares and Foals at Eaton*, and Sir W. Orpen, *2nd Duke of Westminster*

Paul Sweeney, photographer,
   32 Ambleside Road, Flixton, M41 and *Cheshire Life*: *6th Duke of Westminster with the Duchess and their younger children*

Caroline Cust: drawing of a monument formerly in Eccleston church.

Other illustrations are from:

a   The Tate Gallery:
      The Cholmondeley Sisters

b   Public Record Office:
      Chaucer's evidence in the Scrope hearing PRO C 47/6/2

c   Hulton Archive:
      Cliveden; the Drawing Room at Eaton Hall; 2nd Duke with Mlle Coco Chanel; Anne, Duchess of Westminster

d   Country Living/ Art Ashley:
      6th Duke of Westminster

I *The Early Grosvenors (c. 1086–1584)*

When the baby destined to become the first Duke of Westminster was born on 13 October 1825 he was named Hugh Lupus. That name was chosen, no doubt, to stress the longevity of the Grosvenor family's interests in Cheshire. For Hugh Lupus had been the name of William the Conqueror's nephew, the Earl of Chester, who held from the King all the lands of Cheshire (excepting those of the Bishop of Chester) at the end of the eleventh century. The Grosvenors professed to be descended from Hugh Lupus's nephew, Gilbert Grosvenor (*le Gros Veneur* or Master of the Hunt). They were a family who could make a pretty fair claim to have 'come over with the Conqueror'.

OPPOSITE:
Statue at Eaton of Hugh Lupus, first Earl of Chester, by G. F. Watts (1883)

For 400 years Grosvenors of Hulme featured in Cheshire as local governors and upon the wider stage as soldiers fighting for King Edward II against the Scots and for the Black Prince in France. Occasionally they were in full spotlight. In 1385 Sir Robert Grosvenor defended his right to

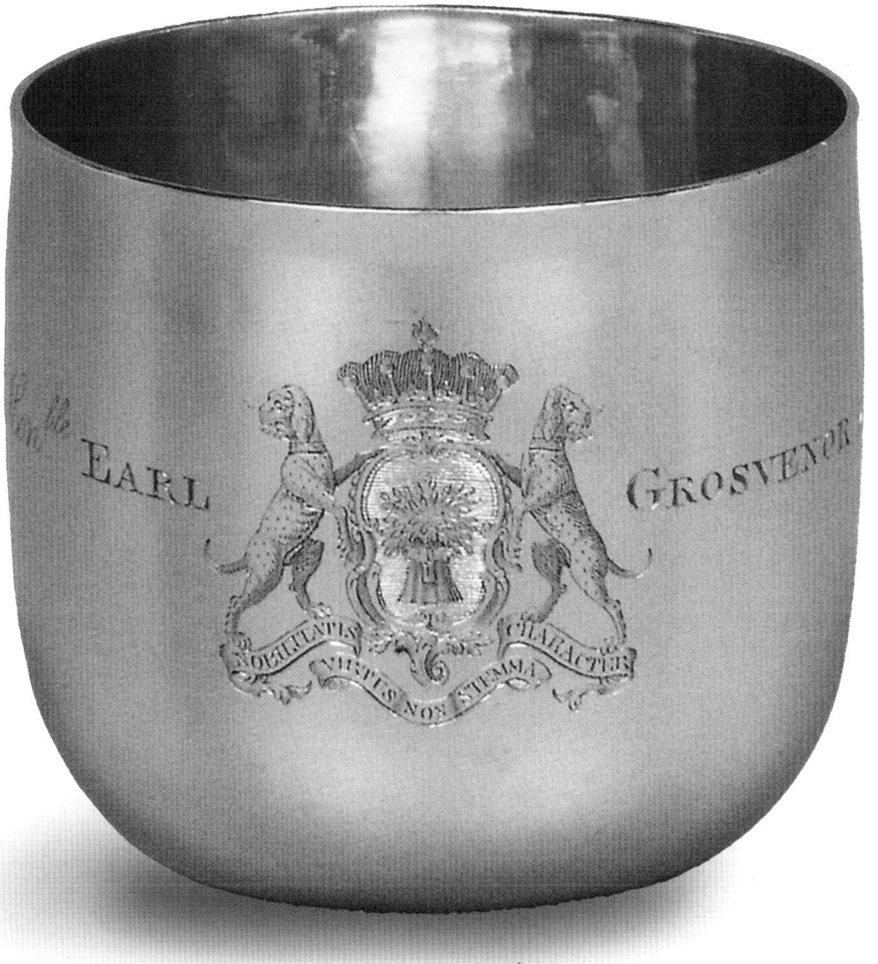
EARL
NOBILITATIS
VIRTUS NON STEMMA
CHARACTER

The arms of Grosvenor: *azure, a garb or* depicted on a gold tumbler cup, presented by Earl Grosvenor as a prize at Chester Races in 1792. The cup was made by Peter and Anne Bateman and incorporates the Grosvenor motto: *Nobilitatis virtus non stemma character.* The supporters to the Grosvenor arms are Talbot dogs.

bear the arms *azure, a bend or* (a golden diagonal band, across a blue shield) against Sir Richard Scrope. The case lasted a full year and was heard by Thomas, Duke of Gloucester and Constable of England. More than 207 knights and gentlemen of Lancashire and Cheshire testified to the use of the *bend or* by Grosvenor and his ancestors. The poet Geoffrey Chaucer recalled seeing Grosvenor's arms hanging outside an inn in Friday Street, London. Nevertheless, the Constable gave judgement against Grosvenor. Sir Robert appealed, necessitating a further trial, heard by King Richard II, who in 1390 confirmed the judgement of the Constable. So Grosvenor adopted new arms: *azure, a garb or* (a golden sheaf on a blue field) – a neat allusion to his claims of kinship with the Earls of Chester.

Sir Robert extended the family's fortunes when he married as his second wife Joan de Pulford. Joan, as the heiress of her brother Thomas, brought landholdings and revenues to the already ample patrimony of the Grosvenors. Their son Thomas married Katherine, daughter and co-heiress of Sir William Phesaunt of Staffordshire, whose second son Ralph (or Rauph) married Joan, heiress of John of Eaton. Thus over three generations the Grosvenors displayed an extraordinary ability to make shrewd and advantageous marriages.

Since Ralph's older brother Robert left six daughters and no heir, the Grosvenor name and fortune continued through Ralph and Joan's descendants while Eaton became the family home on their marriage. Over the next couple of hundred years the Grosvenors amassed one of the most substantial fortunes in the county. On 12 April 1548, for example, Thomas Leigh left the Manor of Belgrave to his wife's family – the Grosvenors. But as well as lands with their manorial rights, the Grosvenors also possessed rights over the river Dee and mineral rights in North Wales.

Geoffrey Chaucer's evidence in the case between Sir Robert Grosvenor and Sir Richard Scrope concerning the right to bear the arms *azure, a bend or*.

2 *Sir Richard Grosvenor, First Baronet (1585–1645)*

Sir Richard was the only surviving son of 17 children. At the age of 10, he travelled the five miles or so to join the large household of John Bruen of Stapleford, a puritan gentleman from whom he received a Protestant education. When he was 13 Richard went up to Queen's College, Oxford – the principal seminary for godly ministers – and graduated four years later with a BA and a firm commitment to Puritan ideals. His public speeches and private letters of advice illustrate his diligent efforts to apply the lessons he learnt at Oxford to his roles as head of his household and local governor. In so doing Richard established himself as 'father of the county', serving as both Justice of the Peace and Member of Parliament for Chester. He made plain the distinction between private interests and public duty when he wrote about the function of an MP:

In our owne perticular occasions wee can bee carefull enough to acte anie thing that may perfect our desires. But shewe mee that man

The Cholmondeley Sisters, (c.1600–1610), from the Tate Gallery. The sisters, one of whom is believed to be Lettice, wife of Sir Richard Grosvenor, gave birth on the same day.

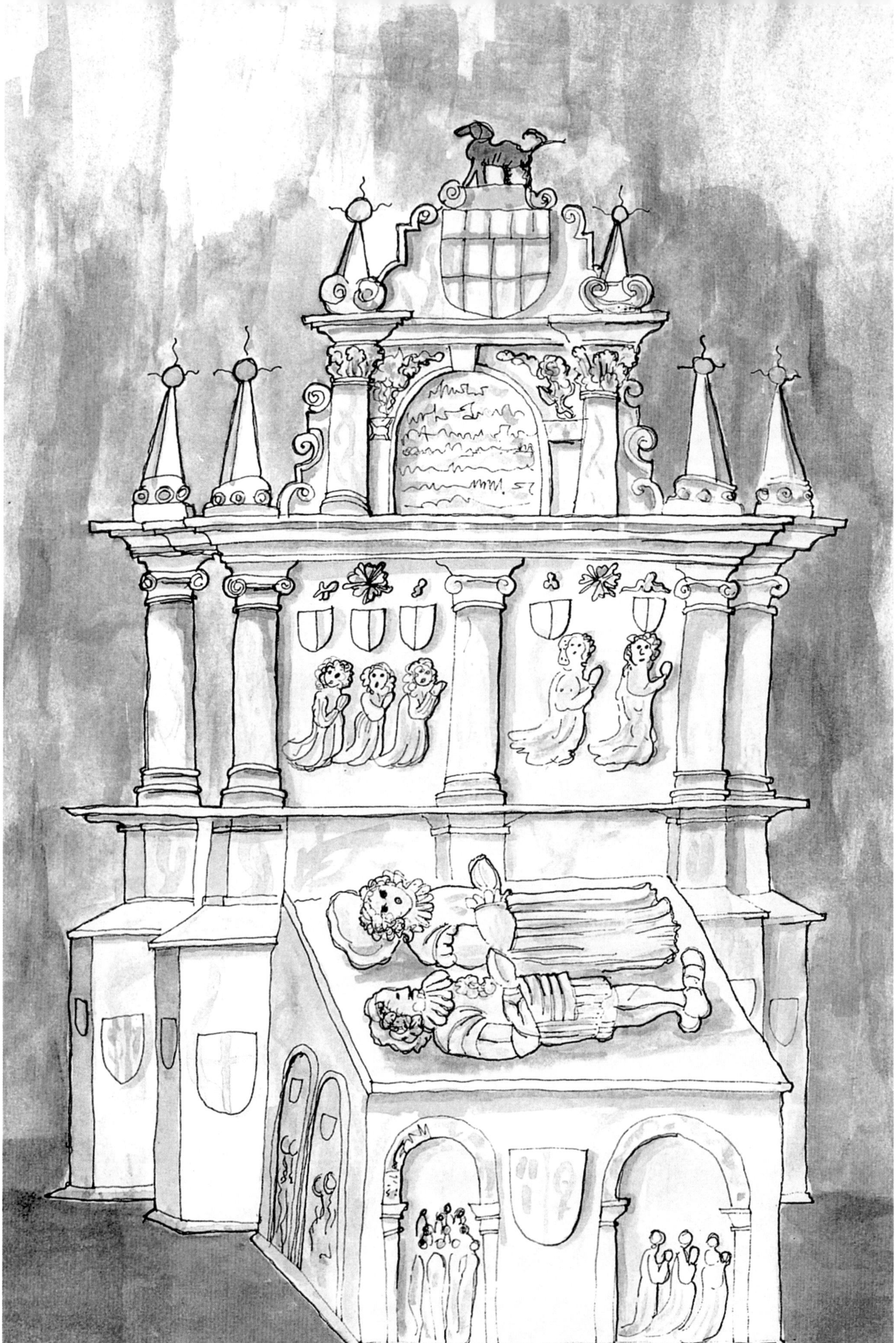

(and I will reverence him) who conceiveth his dutie to bee as greate, and his care as much, for the publique, and whose practice doth second his judgment.

At the age of 15 Richard married Lettice Cholmondeley whose family was ranked second amongst the county elite when the Grosvenor family was ranked fourteenth. The marriage produced four children. Relations between the Cholmondeleys and Grosvenors were close and continued to be so even after Lettice's death in 1612. Richard was on particularly good terms with his mother-in-law Dame Mary and it was at her house, Vale Royal, that Richard was knighted by James I in 1617.

Dame Mary also maintained an interest in her Grosvenor grandchildren. For example, she was eager for her eldest grandson to join the company at Holford, a house situated a couple of miles south west of Knutsford, over the festive season. In a letter that made plain her affection for him, she wrote:

Sir, I pray you give leave to my Sonne [i.e. grandson] *Dick Grosvenor to come to me tomorrow and to be with me the rest of this tyme of Christmas, and to make merry with his Uncles and friends that are now with me. I pray you send him to me for I look for him and am not well without him. And if you had not been a nearer kyn to him than I, you should not have had him all this while.*

In 1614 Richard married Elizabeth Wilbraham from another prominent Cheshire family who lived at Woodhey. Her brother Sir Richard Wilbraham became Richard's closest friend while her half-brother Hugh married Richard's sister, Margaret. After Elizabeth's death in 1621, Richard married Elizabeth Warburton, the widow of Thomas Stanley of Alderley and sole heiress of Sir Peter Warburton, Lord Chief Justice of the Common Pleas. Meanwhile another of Richard's sisters, Christian, married Peter Daniell of Over Tabley and his daughter Christiana married Sir Francis Gamull, later Mayor of Chester. Thus, through his own and his family's marriages, Richard made valuable connections in both the City of Chester and the county of Cheshire. He sat on the magistrate's bench with two of his brothers-in-law, Sir Richard Wilbraham and Peter Daniell.

Peter Daniell soon became a trusted advisor to Richard's family while Richard stood surety for Daniell's debts. But, alas! this connection threatened Richard's carefully constructed matrimonial network and there were catastrophic consequences for him personally, for in 1629 Daniell defaulted on his debts leaving his brother-in-law to spend almost 10 years in the Fleet prison. Richard was painfully conscious of the disgrace to his ancient family name and wrote to the King's principal secretary:

… it were a killing misery for mee to be the overthrow of soe auncient a family as hath continued in Cheshire ever since the Conquest through my too much and foolish kindnes …

However, the crime of debt did not mean Richard was completely

Sir Richard Grosvenor's sumptuous funeral monument, erected in Eccleston church in 1624, defaced in 1642, and since destroyed. It is a conspicuous display of Sir Richard's pride in his ancestry. This sketch is based on the Chester herald Randle Holmes' drawing of 1629.

Sir Richard Grosvenor, First Baronet

incarcerated. The Fleet became his place of residence but he was free to take excursions and dine out in London and further afield. Indeed, he spent much of the period from 1636 to 1638 in Reading where he wined and dined, played cards and bowls and attended church.

Richard kept up correspondence with friends and his family in Cheshire so upon his release from prison – some time after December 1638, when Daniell finally met his debts – Richard was able to resume his position in the county without too much difficulty. Between 1640 and 1642, together with a number of other moderate gentry in Cheshire, he advised restraint and forbearance amid the growing animosity between the King and Parliament. When that failed with the outbreak of the Civil War Richard probably retired quietly to Eaton where he died in September 1645.

Sir Richard Grosvenor, 2nd Bart, depicted in a window in Farndon church.

3 Sir Richard Grosvenor, Second Baronet (c.1604–1665)

The first Baronet was succeeded by his son, also Richard. In November 1628 Richard had married Sydney the daughter of Sir Roger Mostyn of Mostyn, Flintshire, extending the Grosvenor's connections in North Wales. Richard's father could not resist sharing his extensive matrimonial experience with his son. He counselled him to:

> … carry your selfe temperatly & sweetly towards your wife. Love her hartely, use her with all respect, bannish farre from you all harshness. Let her never tast the unwellcome fruit of bitter wordes, nor discover the darke cloudes of discon[ten]ted lookes. And this not onely at the first & while the fayre moone lasteth, but to observe it so longe as you shall keepe you togeather …

When civil war came in 1642, Richard declared for the royalists as did the Cholmondeleys, the Wilbrahams and the Stanleys. He was High Sheriff of Cheshire at the Assizes of February 1643 which outlawed all those who had supported Parliament in the indecisive first battle of the Civil War at Edge Hill the previous October. Following the surrender by the royalists in June 1646 the Committee of Chester interpreted those proceedings as having been part of a 'plot' to murder over a hundred parliamentarians, including the parliamentarian hero, Sir William Brereton, who had held Chester for Parliament in the siege of 1645–1646. Relations between Brereton and Grosvenor plainly were acrimonious for, in his account of the siege, Brereton rather shabbily refers only to Richard's amorous adventures and makes no other mention of his role in Chester.

Richard and his fellow royalists suffered considerable financial hardship for their loyalty to the King. A composition (or fine) was levied based on the capital value of their property that had been sequestrated by Parliament. This was computed at £1,250 for Grosvenor – not as punishing as the hefty £7,742 demanded from Lord Cholmondeley. Further disharmony entered county affairs when efforts to catch those who falsified the value of their estates resulted in Richard being:

> … most unjustly prosecuted upon a Review by one Thomas Mercer which was his tennent, who merely out of spleen & malice hath informed the Commissioners for Compounding etc. that the said Sir Richard hath compounded att an undervalue for his estate …

Richard was a prominent supporter of Sir George Booth's pro-royalist Cheshire and Lancashire Rising in July 1659. However, the rising was abortive and Richard's son and heir, Roger, Cornet Grosvenor, was one of

16 officers and 236 soldiers arrested in August. However, within a year, King Charles II was restored and the political fortunes of the Grosvenors and other royalist families of any note improved considerably.

The celebrations were tragically short-lived at Eaton for, just over a year later, on 22 August 1661, Roger was killed in a duel at Heronbridge by his cousin, Hugh Roberts (of Hafod-y-bwch in Denbigh). The quarrel, which cost Roger his life aged only 33 years, concerned a wager on a servant's footrace. The heir to the Grosvenor estate was Roger's son Thomas who was just eight years old when Richard died on 31 January 1665.

Eaton Hall, designed by William Samwell, and built in the 1670s.

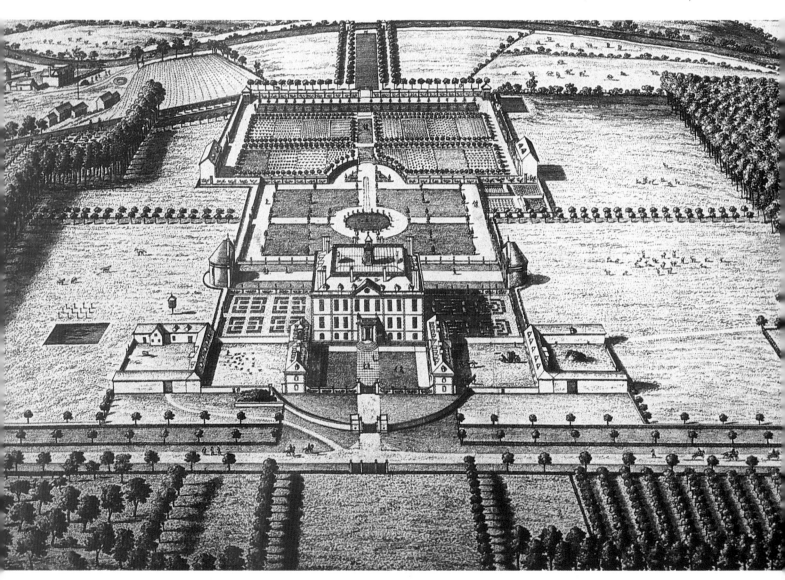

4 Sir Thomas Grosvenor, Third Baronet (1655–1700)

Sir Thomas's birth at midnight on 20 November 1655 was carefully documented by his mother Christian, daughter of Thomas Myddelton of Chirk Castle, in her recipe book – a homely record that reflected the nature of Thomas's upbringing and childhood. Soon after she was widowed Christian married her father's steward, a match that was based on real affection rather than ambition.

At the age of eight Thomas witnessed the awesome ceremony of his grandfather's funeral and listened to the daunting proclamation of his title as Sir Thomas Grosvenor, third Baronet, 'whom God graunt longe to florish.'

Thomas grew up well-endowed and ambitious. Before he was 20 years old he embarked on the task of building a new house for his family. He wanted the house to incorporate features he had seen on youthful travels through Europe and shrewdly he employed the talents of Mr William Samwell, an architect whose credentials included building at Newmarket for the King of England. The finished house was much admired and a traveller to Chester in April 1690 described it thus:

> *I took an elegant walk by the river's side towards Eaton Hall, belonging to Sir Thomas Grosvenor, near which stands a pretty church called Eccleston ... I carried my brother to see Eaton Hall, which is a noble house, square and regular, with many fine walks and trees planted around it, but all new work.*

All this was made possible as a consequence of the soaring Grosvenor fortunes. During the 16th and early 17th centuries the Grovesnors had enjoyed Crown leases of mines and in 1634 they purchased the freehold of lead mines in Coleshill and Rhuddlan in Flintshires and mines of coal, stone and lead in the Lordship of Bromfield and Yale in Denbighshire. Despite the disruption to the Welsh mining industry during the Civil War, these were increasingly productive and were yielding substantial quantities of lead by the 1660s.

Thomas needed a bride to share his new house with him and his choice was Mary Davies who was twelve years old and possessed of an estate composed of pasture, arable and swamp to the west of London. The property was part of the Manor of Eia which had belonged to Westminster Abbey before passing into secular hands during the reign of Henry VIII. In 1626, it was owned by Hugh Awdeley, the son of a mercer, who sold pieces of it to wealthy courtiers wishing to build houses away from London's congested streets.

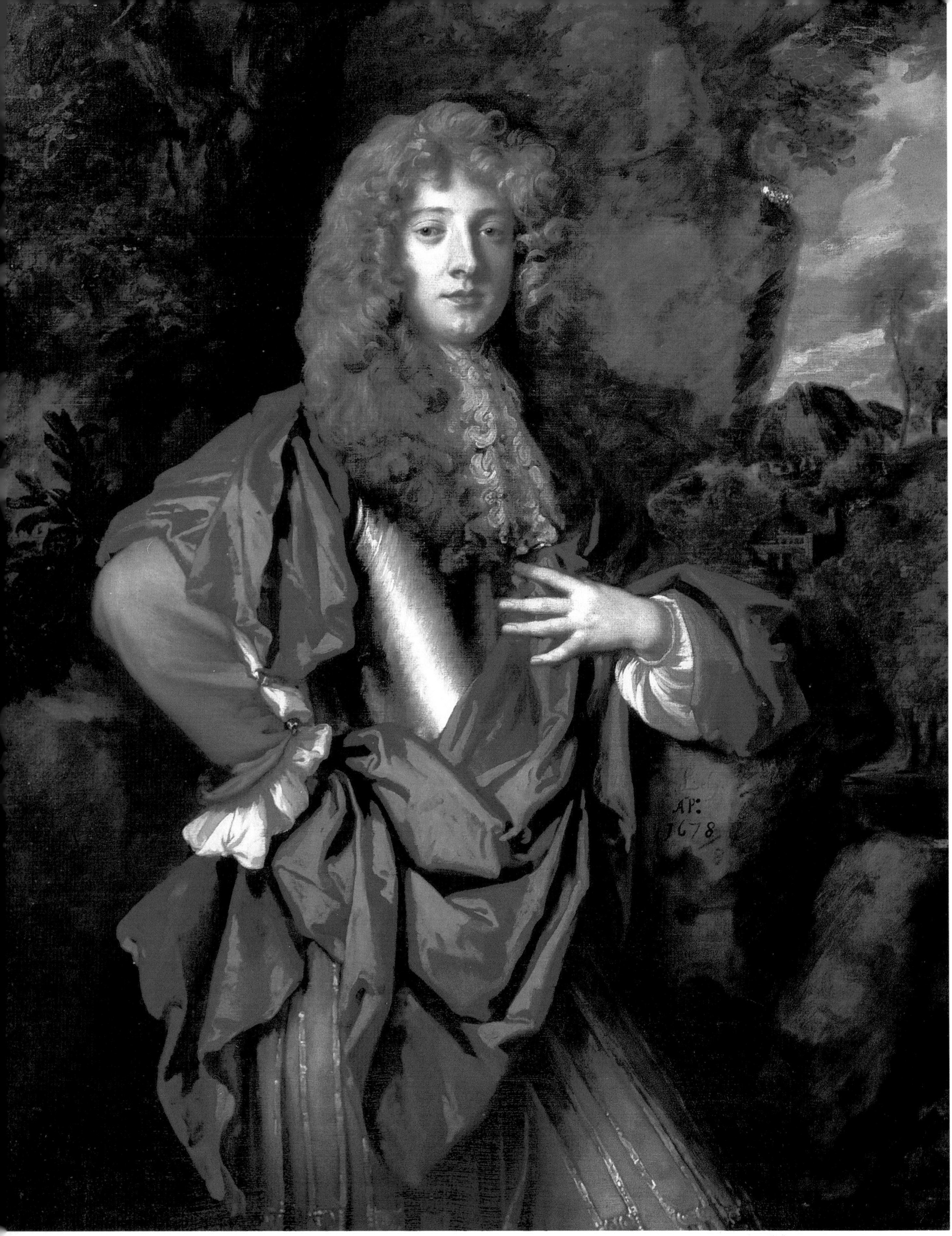
AP:
1678

Mary Davies, Lady Grosvenor, by Michael Dahl. Twelve-year-old Mary's marriage to the 21-year-old Sir Thomas Grosvenor in 1677 brought to the family 'swampy meads' outside London.

Upon his death in 1662, the childless Hugh Awdeley divided his estate amongst the grandsons of his sister with the least attractive part – the 'swampy meads' of the Manor of Ebury – passing to Alexander Davies, 'scrivener', who died three years later. Alexander's daughter Mary inherited two-thirds of his fortune and his 21-year-old widow inherited a third. Remarried to John Tregonwell, Mary's mother set about managing an estate crippled by her first husband's mismanagement but which clearly had potential. There was also the task of finding a husband for little Mary.

The heiress was brought up by her aunt in a 'faire mansion house' at Millbank and she was paraded in a carriage drawn by six horses. A first match fell through and Mrs. Tregonwell selected a bridegroom from amongst the country gentry with a long pedigree, a title and a fortune that was more than double that of Mary's. For in the 1670s Mary Davies's inheritance had only just begun to realize its potential and the streets and squares of Mayfair and Belgravia were not yet dreamed of. On 10 October 1677 the 12-year-old Mary was married to Sir Thomas Grosvenor, Bart., aged 21 years. The disparity in their ages betokens the fact that this was primarily a business arrangement.

Thomas brought his bride to her new home at Eaton when she was about 15 and thereafter they divided their time between Cheshire and London. Relations between them were affectionate and they had six children of which four survived into adulthood. Thomas served as Mayor of Chester and was an active MP for Chester in six parliaments.

The Protestant Thomas loyally defended the Catholic James II for as long as his conscience would allow – even to the extent of raising and commanding a troop of horse on the King's behalf – but after King James was replaced by King William Thomas was accused of harbouring Jacobite sympathies.

That Thomas could be suspected of pro-Catholic sentiments was no doubt a consequence of his wife's conversion to Catholicism shortly after her arrival in Cheshire. She had been introduced to the Romish faith by a young man, William Massey of Puddington Hall on Wirral. In itself, the new Lady Grosvenor's conversion should not have presented a problem for Thomas for in English minds there had long been a distinction between Catholicism and popery, the one generally tolerated and the other an object of fear and loathing. But in the late seventeenth century in a fevered atmosphere of popish plots and of conflict between James II and William III suspicions were easily whipped up. Doubts about his loyalty cast a shadow over the last years of Thomas's life, while matters were made worse by Mary who was showing clear signs of mental illness. Thomas died, and

Sir Thomas Grosvenor, 3rd Bart, by Sir Peter Lely.

Sir Thomas Grosvenor, Third Baronet

was buried on 2 July 1700, having left his sons to the care of Sir Richard Myddelton of Chirk and the brothers Thomas and Francis Cholmondeley, of Vale Royal – undoubted Protestants.

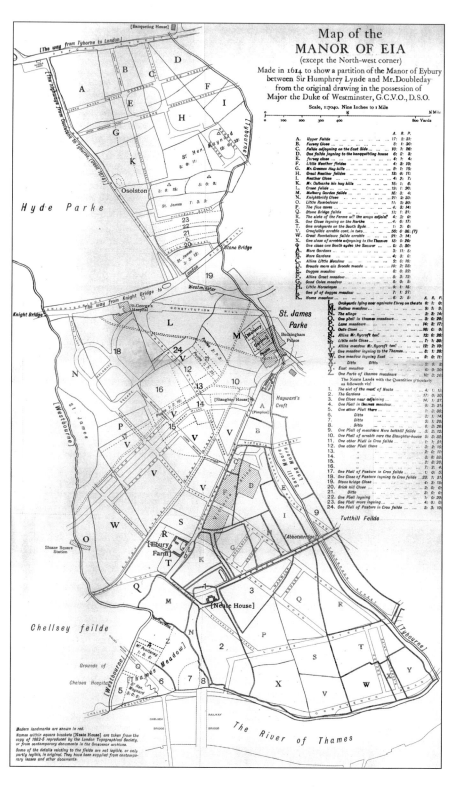

The Manor of Eia, Mary Davies' inheritance showing, in red, the streets developed on the former meadows.

5 Sir Richard Grosvenor, Fourth Baronet (1689–1732); Sir Thomas Grosvenor, Fifth Baronet (1693–1733); Sir Robert Grosvenor, Sixth Baronet (1695–1755)

Sir Thomas Grosvenor was succeeded in the baronetcy by all three of his sons. The eldest, Richard, was still at Eton when his father died, after which he went on the Grand Tour to Switzerland, Bavaria, Italy and the Netherlands. He finally came home in 1707 and the following year, at the age of 19, he married 18-year-old Jane, daughter of Sir Edward Wyndham, Bart., of Orchard-Wyndham.

According to the House of Lords' records she was married with the consent of her guardian, Lord Gower. Sir Richard and Jane had a daughter Catherine, who died in 1718. When Jane died the following year, Richard married Diana, only daughter of Sir George Warburton of Arley (between Knutsford and Warrington). Sadly, this marriage produced no children.

In 1715 Richard took his seat as MP for Chester. This was the year of the Jacobite rising in favour of the Old Pretender and the Grosvenors were part of a group who drank toasts to the 'king over the water' (James Stuart, son of the deposed King James II). In September, Richard had attended a meeting of the Jacobite Cheshire Club which decided against taking part in the rebellion. The following month he was elected Mayor and chose to remain in Chester rather than to sit in Parliament in Westminster, for Chester was volatile and under martial law.

Sir Richard successfully petitioned for the restoration of civil law but his loyalty remained suspect. For instance, his name appeared on a list of Jacobite leaders sent to the Pretender in 1721 and in 1730 he was in correspondence with the Stuart court in Rome. Even so, in 1727 he had participated in the coronation of the Hanoverian king George II. In the General Election of that year Sir Richard and his brother Thomas won both parliamentary seats giving the Grosvenors outright control of Chester for the first time.

In 1704, the Grosvenors' Welsh lead mines had

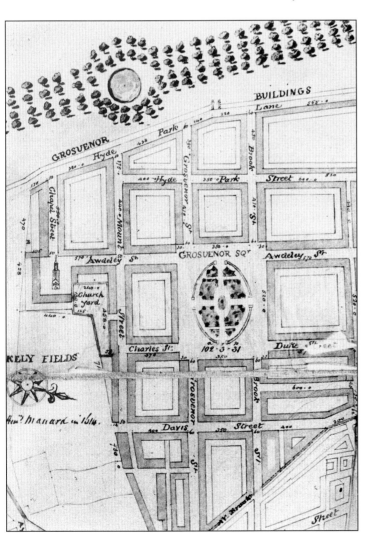

Mayfair in 1723. John Mackay's plan of streets recently laid out.

Grosvenor Square, looking north, 1730–35.

been leased to the London Lead Company ensuring that the family benefited from long-term planning and investment at a time when mining generally was regarded as a quick profit-making 'adventure'. The income from the mines made possible further development of the Grosvenor estate in London. An article in the Daily Post, dated 12 July 1725, described how:

> *The several new streets in Grosvenor Buildings in the Parish of St George, Hanover Square, and lying between Bond Street and Hyde Park were last week particularly named: upon which occasion Sir Richard Grosvenor, Bart. gave a very splendid entertainment to his tenants and others concerned with those buildings ... In the centre of those new buildings there is now making a square called Grosvenor Square [with gardens designed by William Kent], which for its largeness and beauty will far exceed any yet made in or about London.*

Eaton Hall also continued to attract admiration. On 10 September 1731, one Mrs Pendarves wrote to her sister Mrs Ann Grenville from Chester, *en route* to Ireland. She had visited Sir Richard Grosvenor's house:

> *... where we were mightily pleased with the place; the gardens are laid*

out in the old-fashioned taste, with cut-work parterres, and wilderness enclosed in hedges; the grounds lie extremely well to the house, and everywhere there is a fine prospect. We were offered fruit and wine, though Sir Richard Grosvenor was not there …

There is an account of Richard racing his horses at Chester and Newmarket, in 1720. This is the first record of the Grosvenors' association with the turf – an attachment that endures to the present day.

In July 1732 Richard died and was succeeded by his brother, Thomas. Thomas, being very ill, was advised to travel to Italy and he died in Naples the following February. Accordingly, the youngest son, Robert, became the sixth Baronet. He had followed his brothers to Eton before going up to Brasenose College, Oxford and then to the Inner Temple in London. In May 1730 he married Jane, daughter and heiress of John Warre of Swell Court and Shepton-Beauchamp in Somerset. The bride and groom shared a grandmother in Mrs Tregonwell. Their first son, Richard, was born on 18 June 1731 followed by a second son in March 1734 and four daughters. For a while Robert's interests moved to Somerset but upon assuming the Baronetcy he returned to Eaton where he won a parliamentary seat comfortably.

The old Tory/Jacobite associations returned to haunt Robert in 1745 with the second rebellion, this time in support of the Young Pretender, and there were rumours that he was to join the rebels in Lancashire. In fact, Robert was being presented at court before returning to Chester later that year to assist preparations for the defence of the city. Indeed, he donated £2,000 towards a subscription to raise and maintain men for the King's service with the promise of the same again if it were needed. Moreover, he went on to become one of the prominent Tories who were closely identified with the Prince of Wales.

When he died in August 1755 his younger son Thomas was returned as MP without a poll, despite his extreme youth (he was just 21) and the fact that his older brother Richard held the other seat. The Grosvenor hegemony in Chester politics was complete.

Mares and Foals at Eaton, by George Stubbs, commissioned by Sir Richard Grosvenor, First Earl Grosvenor

The Fourth, Fifth and Sixth Baronets

6 Richard Grosvenor, Seventh Baronet, Baron Grosvenor, Earl Grosvenor, Viscount Belgrave (1731–1802)

The new Baronet and his brother Thomas were politically active at the very highest levels. They dined regularly with George Grenville the First Minister and were supporters of Pitt. That Richard Grosvenor was also accounted to be one of the most prominent members of the fashionable set is demonstrated in a letter from Horace Walpole wherein he recommended that '… if you propose a fashionable assembly you must send cards to Lord Spenser and Lord Grosvenor …'

Richard was gripped by two great passions: horse racing and art collecting. His name appeared frequently among the lists of purchasers in England and abroad when he employed King George II's librarian and keeper of antiquities to buy paintings in Florence. His enthusiasm for horses and racing was graphically illustrated by Walpole's wry account of his creation as Baron Grosvenor in April 1761. Referring to a number of new peers he explained that Richard Grosvenor has been created '… a

Sir Richard Grosvenor, First Earl Grosvenor, by Sir Joshua Reynolds (attr.). Sir Richard's passions were art-collecting and horse racing.

BELOW:
The Grosvenor Hunt, Eaton, by
George Stubbs. Those to the right are
(from the left): Thomas Grovesnor;
Richard, Lord Grovesnor (on Honest
John); unknown; Sir Roger Mostyn,
Bt,; Peter Thomas (Huntsman) and Mr
Bell Lloyd. The others in green livery
are hunt servants.

viscount or baron, I don't know which, nor does he for yesterday when he should have kissed [the king's] hands, he was gone to Newmarket to see the trial of a race horse …' He clearly was a good judge of horseflesh for his horses won the Derby three times and the Oaks six. There were Grosvenor studs at Wallasey in Wirral and at Eaton where Richard's two passions were given expression by George Stubbs in his lovely painting of mares and foals in the Eaton paddock.

Relations between the late Sir Robert and his younger son, Thomas,

The Seventh Baronet

seem to have been strained. He left him just one thousand pounds a year, in land. This provoked the dowager Lady Grosvenor to express some dissatisfaction, Thomas having been her favourite. Richard immediately presented his brother with £10,000 demanding neither thanks nor recognition.

Richard married Henrietta, the daughter of Lady Harriet and Mr Henry Vernon, the Commissioner of Excise, having announced his intention to Grenville who was dining with him and his brother. They married on 19 July 1764. It was a match that was to provide one of the most sensational scandals of the day with wide ranging repercussions in court and government. Henrietta Grosvenor moved in the highest circles and was frequently seen at Lady Cowper's ultra-fashionable assemblies at Richmond where another regular visitor was King George III's youngest brother, Henry, Duke of Cumberland. Henrietta, aged 24, and Cumberland, aged 28, soon engaged in an affair. The polite world was rocked

Sir Thomas Grosvenor as a boy. As an MP Sir Thomas was a supporter of William Pitt.

OPPOSITE:
Henrietta Vernon, Lady Grosvenor, wife of Sir Richard. Her relationship with the Duke of Cumberland, the king's son, led to a sensational court case.
Portrait by Thomas Gainsborough

LEFT:
Sir Thomas Grosvenor, by George Romney.

18

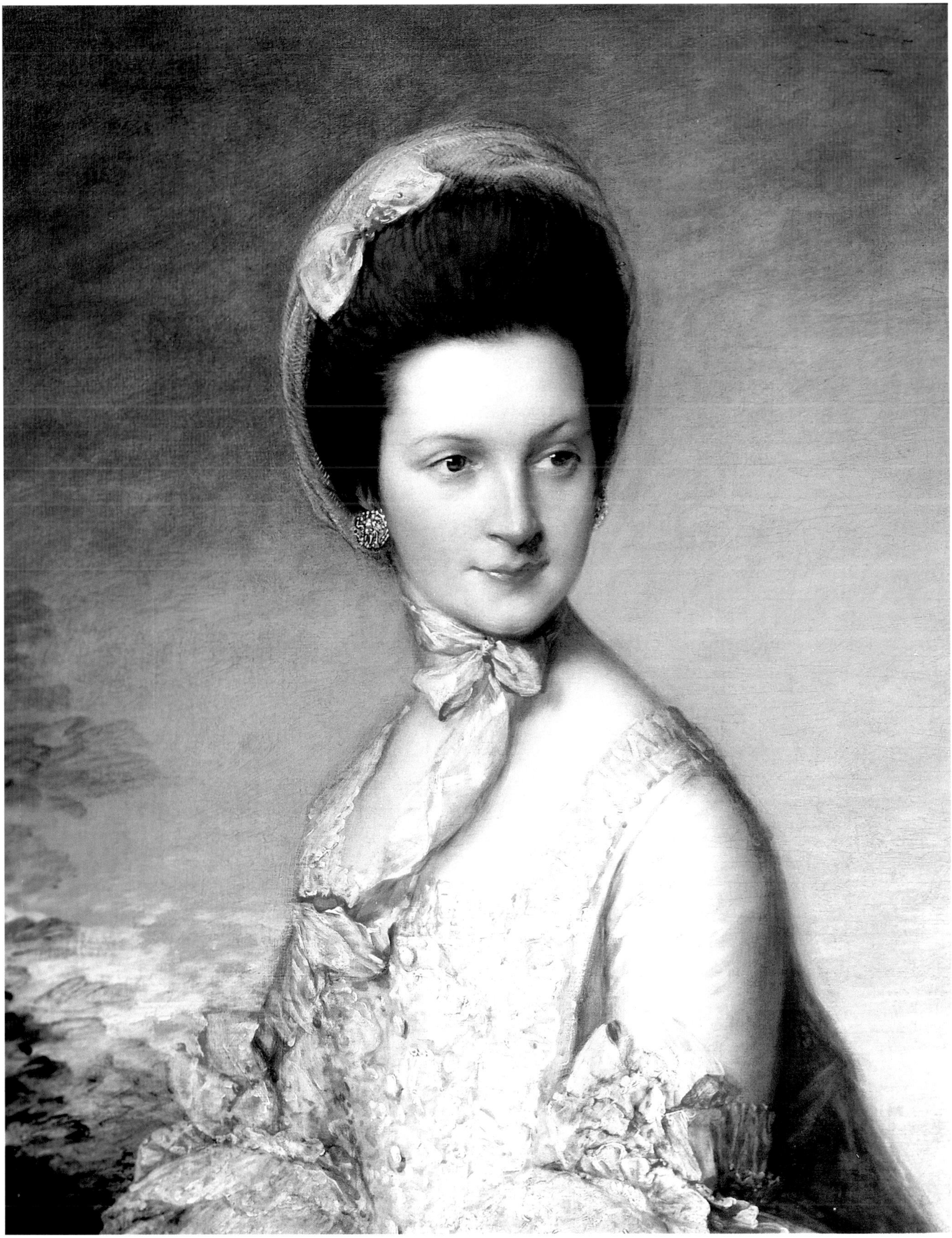

when Lord Grosvenor 'exhibited a libel against his wife for adultery' with the Duke of Cumberland in March 1770. Lord Grosvenor was awarded £10,000 damages from the Duke of Cumberland in respect of his 'criminal conversation' with Henrietta. Together with costs, Lord Grosvenor stood to gain the staggering sum of £13,000. As a postscript to the matter, upon mention of horned cattle during the reading of the King's address to the House of Lords, Lord Grosvenor and the Duke of Grafton, who had recently divorced his wife, stood up and solemnly bowed to each other. Lord Grosvenor generously settled £1,200 a year on his estranged wife. Upon his death, thirty years later, she married General George Porter, Baron de Hochepied, MP, and lived on until 1828 when she was over 80.

Meanwhile, Lord Grosvenor's brother Thomas continued as MP for Chester. By now the Grosvenors' stranglehold on Chester politics had provoked a rival parliamentary candidate, John Crewe, to bemoan that 'any opposition to [the Grosvenor family] is now considered as little less than a rebellion by the lawful authority.' Thomas Grosvenor was regarded as the informal leader of the independent country gentleman and he was a firm supporter of Pitt. That Pitt perceived Lord Grosvenor to be a valuable political ally is demonstrated in his recommendation that Lord Grosvenor be created Viscount Belgrave and Earl Grosvenor, in 1784. Thomas Grosvenor died on 12 February 1795 and Richard Grosvenor, Earl Grosvenor, on 5 August 1802.

Robert, Viscount Belgrave, later First Marquess of Westminster, by Thomas Gainsborough. Robert developed Belgravia and Pimlico.

7 Robert Grosvenor, Second Earl Grosvenor, First Marquess of Westminster (1767–1845)

Robert, First Marquess of Westminster
by John Jackson.

Robert Grosvenor was aged thirty-five when he succeeded his father to the Earldom. When his parents were engaged in their messy court case he had been a toddler. He was educated at Westminster, Harrow and Trinity College, Cambridge before making his Grand Tour between 1786 and 1788. On 28 April 1794 he married the Honourable Eleanor Egerton, the only child of Sir Thomas Egerton, who was created Earl of Wilton in 1801. Eleanor was later described by her daughter-in-law, Lady Elizabeth Grosvenor, as kind and dutiful though far from stimulating company. The couple's first son, Richard, Lord Belgrave, was born in 1795. A second son Thomas was born four years later, who assumed his maternal grandfather's title upon his death in 1814. Another son, Robert, was born in 1801, followed by a daughter, Amelia, who died in her early teens.

As well as his father's titles, fortune and Tory allegiances, Robert also inherited his artistic taste and enthusiasm for horse racing. He made many notable additions to his father's collection of pictures, paying fabulous sums such as £10,000 for four canvases by Rubens and just £100 for Gainsborough's Blue Boy. He bred and owned many good horses while his cousin General Grosvenor bred the charger Copenhagen that carried the Duke of Wellington through the Battle of Waterloo. A rumour that Robert meant to sell his stud and quit the turf was revealed as false when important parliamentary debates were delayed by his absences at Newmarket.

Although he was a staunch supporter of Pitt Robert joined the Whigs upon Pitt's death, maintaining a liberal Whig view for the rest of his life. His principles led him to befriend the victims of the 'Peterloo' massacre in Manchester and to support such causes as Catholic Emancipation and the abolition of the Corn Laws. In particular he was firm supporter of the Reform Bill that aimed to extend the franchise and redistribute parliamentary seats to ensure better representation – even though this would be detrimental to his personal interests. He was appointed Lord of the Admiralty, Privy Councillor and Knight of the Garter. On the other hand, Robert was not afraid to champion Queen Caroline against her husband King George IV; he was apparently driven to throw the Prayer Book or Bible (accounts vary) at the King's head, jeopardizing his political career. And when the City of Chester bestowed the freedom of the city upon the Duke of Wellington he refused to allow Chester Town Hall to be used for the event.

Robert created a fashionable new residential quarter around Belgravia and Pimlico, near Buckingham House that was being rebuilt as a royal

The façade of Grosvenor House.

OPPOSITE:
The drawing room at Eaton Hall.

palace. By appointing Thomas Cundy, and then his son, as architect and surveyor, and Thomas Cubitt, a speculative builder of outstanding merit, he ensured that the development was solidly and superbly constructed. Robert also turned his attention to providing himself with a suitable London residence. The Grosvenors' town house had been part of Alexander Davies's original seventeenth century development of Millbank but in 1806 Robert acquired a great house in Upper Grosvenor Street. He carried out extensive alterations and within two years had created a house that caused Lady Sarah Spencer to declare that 'the vast quantities of beauties of Grosvenor House surpassed all expectations.' In 1827 a magnificent picture gallery was added to the Park Lane side of the house and in 1843 a new entrance was built in Upper Grosvenor Street consisting of a façade of classical pillars between two large gateways.

At Eaton Hall Robert built a huge new mansion on the site of Samwell's house. He chose as its architect William Porden, already known to him as surveyor of the London estate. Originally, it was expected the job would take two years and cost £10,000. A little less than 10 years later the cost had risen to over £100,000 and still the house was not finished. The result was a house that took the relatively modest gothic style to dizzying heights of flamboyance and splendour – or which plumbed the depths of vulgarity and bad taste – depending on one's point of view. Samwell's Caroline house was encased in a gothic facing of light coloured stone which incorporated every possible permutation of the gothic style: turrets, pinnacles, pointed windows, octagonal towers and buttresses – both regular and

OPPOSITE:
William Porden's gothic Eaton Hall, built for the First Marquess.

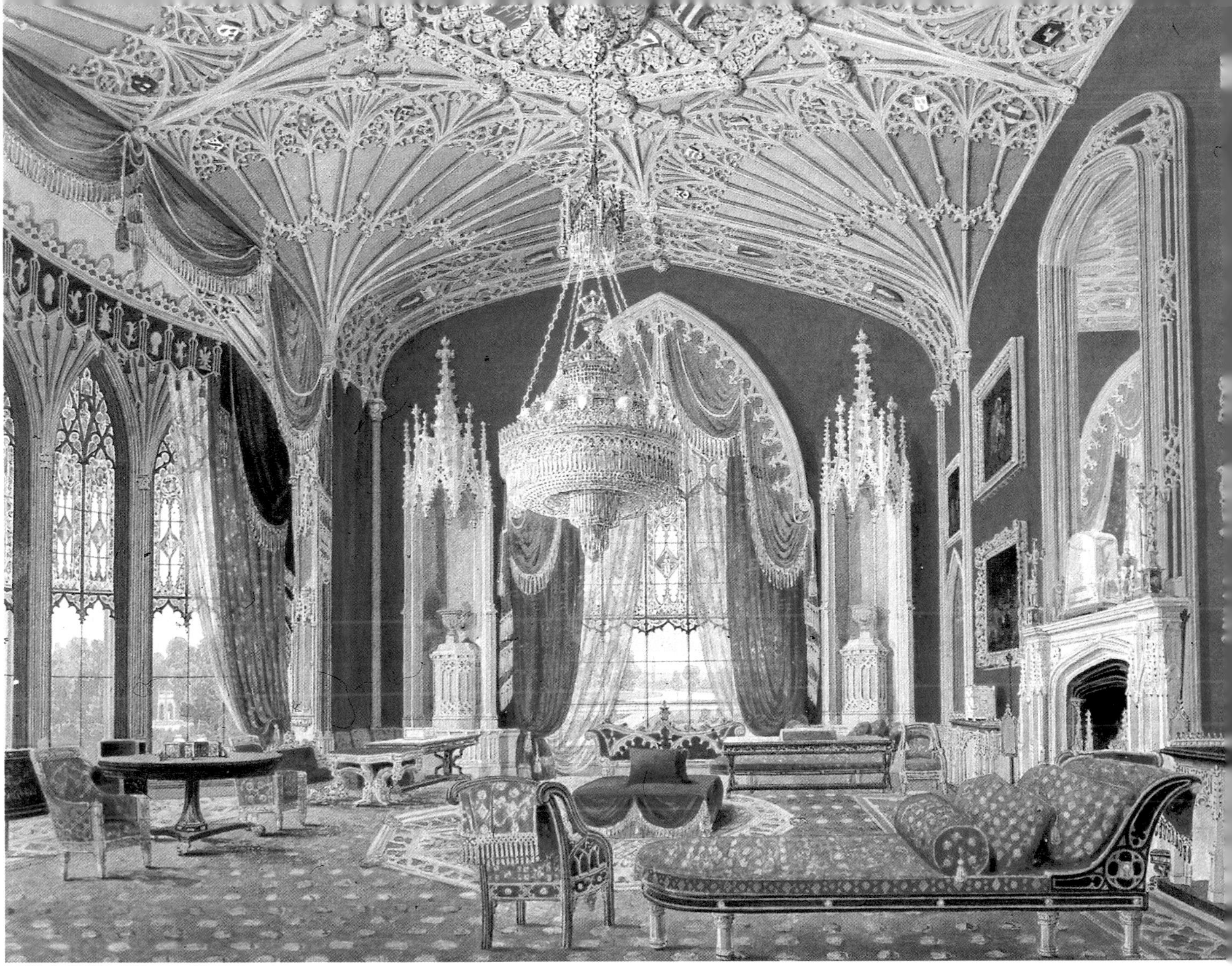

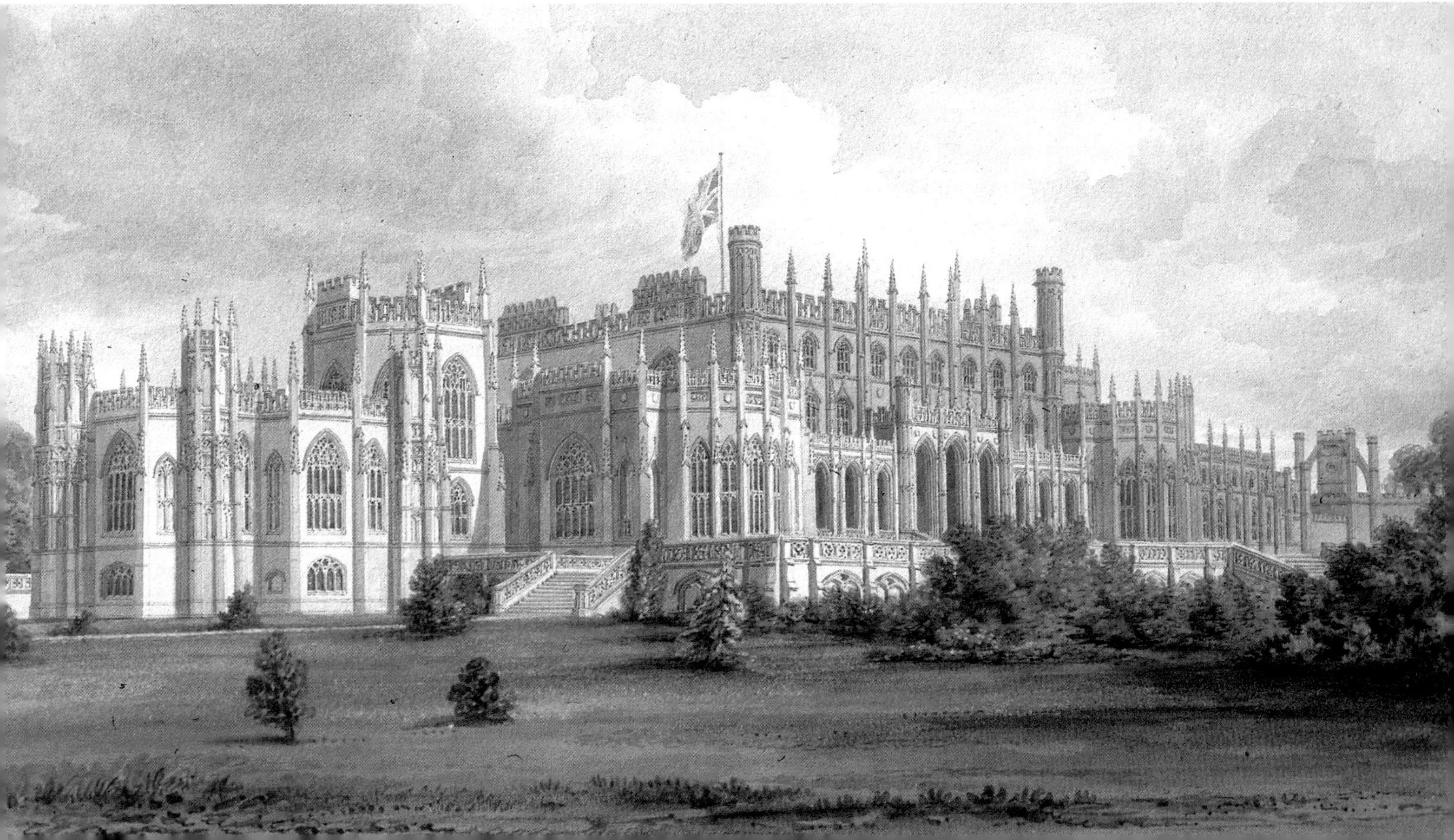

flying. Four new wings were built. The interior of the house was as extravagant and opulent as the very latest upholsterer-decorators could make it. One of its most enthusiastic admirers was the thriteen-year-old Princess Victoria who visited Eaton with her mother in 1832. She wrote in her journal:

The house is magnificent. You drive up to the door under a lofty vaulted portico with a flight of steps under it and it takes you to the hall, which is beautiful. The floor is inlaid with various marbles, and arches spring up from the sides. Then you enter a beautiful drawing room. The ceiling joins in a round, gilt with great taste and richness, while the sides arch towards the top. An organ on the right as you enter the room and a large fireplace on the left, and stained glass windows. The breakfast room is magnificent. There are four fireplaces and the windows are of stained glass, very beautifully done. A massive lustre of gold with an eagle likewise in gold hangs from the ceiling in the middle of the room.

Others described the new Eaton Hall as 'the most gaudy concern I ever saw' or condemned it out of hand as 'a vast pile of mongrel gothic which ... is a monument of wealth, ignorance and bad taste'.

Robert maintained the family interest in horse racing and expanded the Eaton stud. Most remarkable of the horses he bred was Touchstone, who won 16 of the 21 races for which he was started, including the St Leger and two Ascot and two Doncaster Gold Cups. In twenty years Touchstone sired 323 winners of over 700 races. Robert also invested in land, buying the neighbouring Pulford estate in 1813. Later, he bought estates in Dorset, Hampshire and Hertfordshire.

Relations now between the Grosvenors and the royal family were much more correct. Robert was created Marquess of Westminster in King William IV's Coronation Honours in 1831, and he participated in Queen Victoria's Coronation in 1837 with his little grandson Hugh Lupus as his page. He died in February 1845 at Eaton. Lady Elizabeth, the wife of his eldest son, described the funeral cortege as it left for Eccleston church thus:

Above 100 tenants and the clergymen of Lord Westminster's livings – about 8 of them – came to breakfast. At 11½ the procession set forth and was very melancholy and impressive, consisting of the tenants on foot, seven mourning coaches, containing Grosvenor, Wilton, Robert, Hugh, and Gilbert, the clergymen and upper servants, gardener, bailiff, stud groom and steward. Then came Lord Westminster's coach and four, followed by the servants on foot. Lady Westminster saw it all with me from the window of the school room. The Park was filled with people who came from Liverpool.

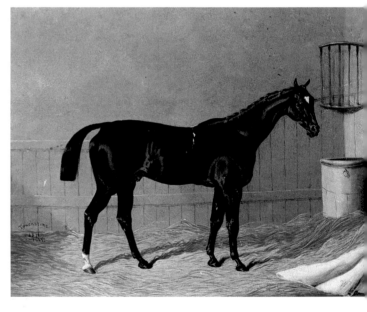

Touchstone. He won 16 of the 21 races for which he was started and sired 323 winning racehorses.

8 *Richard Grosvenor, Third Earl Grosvenor, Second Marquess of Westminster (1795–1869)*

Richard, Viscount Belgrave, later Second Marquess, by John Russell.

Richard Grosvenor, Viscount Belgrave, studied at Westminster and Christ Church College, Oxford before embarking on a Grand Tour of Europe in 1815. His parents devoted much loving care to him and his brothers and instilled in them high moral principles, which stayed with Robert for the whole of his life. In 1818, aged 23, he was elected MP for Chester. The following year, he married the 22-year-old Lady Elizabeth Leveson-Gower, the younger daughter of the second Marquess of Stafford who in 1833 was created first Duke of Sutherland. The Leveson-Gowers were of an ancient Yorkshire family which had estates in Staffordshire and Scotland and were even wealthier than the Grosvenors. Upon his death in 1833, Elizabeth Grosvenor's father was described by Charles Greville as 'a Leviathan of wealth; I believe the richest individual who ever died'.

Once married, Richard and Elizabeth lived at Eaton with Lord and Lady Grosvenor. Between 1820 and 1840 they had 13 children of whom 10 survived to adulthood – all of them into their seventies and two into their nineties. In 1823 an heir was born, Gilbert, who died before he was a year old. Then, in October 1825, Hugh Lupus was born at Eaton. The arrival was greeted rapturously and the christening, in Eccleston Church, was lavish and splendid.

The Belgraves spent their time at Eaton visiting or being visited by friends and relations and engaging in country pursuits such as hunting and fishing. Richard also fulfilled his obligations to local government in his capacity as a Justice of the Peace and to central government when he sat in the House of Commons. Accordingly, each April the entire Grosvenor family moved to London where they remained for the 'season' occupying several houses in Grosvenor Square. There they joined fashionable society in a nightly round of dinners and balls and the theatre. In 1827 they toured Norway, Sweden and Russia and in 1835–36 they travelled through Germany and Italy.

In 1831, with Robert, Lord Grosvenor being created Marquess of

Richard, Viscount Belgrave, later
Second Marquess, by Henry Pickersgill.

Westminster, Richard and Elizabeth assumed the names of Earl and
Countess Grosvenor and Hugh, aged six, became Viscount Belgrave. They
acquired a house of their own, at Motcombe in Dorset – part of the estate
that had been purchased by his father – which was thoroughly refurbished
before they moved into it with their nine children in 1833. When in
London, they frequently visited the Duchess of Kent and her daughter
Princess Victoria, and they were among the first to dine with Victoria at
Buckingham Palace when she became Queen in 1837. After the Marquess's
death in 1845 Richard and Elizabeth assumed the titles of Marquess and
Marchioness and moved into Grosvenor House while in London and into
Eaton for the rest of the year. They began making the house at Eaton more
comfortable almost immediately with the assistance of William Burn. The
new Marquess took his seat in the House of Lords while Hugh represented
Chester in the House of Commons.

The Marquess and Marchioness entertained on a grand scale in London
with dinner parties that included members of the British and foreign royal
families, followed by evening parties for an many as 400 people.
Meanwhile, the Marquess added steadily to his Dorset and Cheshire properties, where he was a model landlord. In 1869, at the age of 74, the
Marquess died after a short illness, leaving his widow utterly devastated.
He was buried in the family vault at Eccleston Church. With the help of
her youngest daughter Theodora, the Dowager Marchioness built up a life
of her own and lived on to within a month of her 94th birthday.

9 *Hugh Lupus Grosvenor, First Duke of Westminster (1825–1899)*

Hugh Lupus was forty-four years old when he succeeded his father. Educated at Eton and Balliol he was affable and gracious. His father had attended to his moral education: duty must be put before pleasure, wealth never used for ostentation or extravagance. The Marquess advised Hugh even after he had married at the age of twenty-six:

> *Your habits are expensive and you live in expensive society ... with only a life interest in this strictly curtailed property I am sorry I cannot aid you, and, as I warned you the other day, I have not a sixpence in the funds.*

Relenting, the next year he granted Hugh £10,000.

For his bride Hugh chose Lady Constance Leveson-Gower, his 17-year-old first cousin, daughter of the Duke of Sutherland. The Queen attended the wedding, for Constance's mother, 'dear Harriet', was a favourite and Mistress of the Robes. Victoria confided in her journal that of her sisters Constance was 'the only one really like her mother and has just the same deep voice'. She was interested in all Constance's eight children and described the oldest boy Victor as 'my dear little godson' and later as 'the greatest darling possible, so pretty and so wonderfully forward and amusing.'

Constance laughed exuberantly, flashed with gaiety and became an enchanting hostess. To Oscar Wilde she was 'the most fascinating, Circe-like, brilliant woman I have ever met in England, something too charming'. Lord Esher described the entrance to one of the great balls at Grosvenor House:

> *As you passed through the outer rooms, from the walls of which Gainsboroughs looked down, and entered the ball-room decorated by Rubens, the fragrance of the flowers was almost overpowering. If you were early you would be greeted by the ample welcome of Constance, and a gracious salutation from the grave seigneur who was her husband.*

Eaton was the couple's country base. With an income of over £60,000 a year Hugh could afford to commission Alfred Waterhouse to replace Porden's building with a new gothic palace. Work began in 1870 and the project took twelve years to complete. It cost £803,000, so sumptuous were Hugh's decorative requirements. Stacey Marks painted a frieze of the Canterbury Pilgrims in the morning room, Gertrude Jekyll created a series of panels for the drawing room, and other rooms were hung with paintings

Constance, Duchess of Westminster,
by Sir John Everett Millais.

Hugh Lupus, First Duke of
Westminster, by Sir John Everett
Millais, 1872.

Cliveden, built for the Duke of Sutherland, inherited by his daughter Constance, Duchess of Westminster.

by Gainsborough, Stubbs and Reynolds. The library was 90 feet long, the dining room with its ante room a hundred and five feet, the Great Hall octagonal. 'Good God!' a guest later exclaimed on entering the vaulted breakfast room, 'I never expected to eat bacon and eggs in a cathedral!' A clock tower 183 feet high housed a carillon of twenty-eight bells. There was an organ in the chapel, another in the hall. Gas was installed and, in 1887, an electricity supply added. The Telegraph described the building as 'one of the most princely and beautiful mansions that these islands contain.'

The Hall would accommodate parties of up to four dozen guests who stayed for a few days, feasted, sported with guns or on horseback, attended races or some other festivity and admired horses in the paddocks. A staff of 35 dusted, lit coal fires, prepared lamps and carried water for baths. There were 13 girls in the laundry, a French chef and kitchen staff, 70 men under the head forester, 40 gardeners and seven on the Hall's special Fire Brigade. In total, Eaton's staff exceeded 300. Hugh believed it was his duty to affect a style that reflected his wealth and social position.

Aside from all these domestic concerns, in 1860 Hugh formed the Queen's Westminster Rifle Volunteers of which he became Lieutenant Colonel. The Cheshire Yeomanry he led as Colonel Commandant from 1869. His temperament politically was liberal though laced with independence. He assumed a leading role in the House in the 1860s when he

The First Duke of Westminster

ABOVE:
Eaton Hall, designed by Alfred
Waterhouse, completed in 1882.

LEFT:
The Library at Eaton Hall.

OPPOSITE:
The Drawing Room at Eaton Hall.

31   *The First Duke of Westminster*

Some of the three hundred staff at the Hall.

moved an amendment to the Whig leader Gladstone's Reform Bill that was seconded by Lord Stanley, son of the leader of the Tories. 'A pair of selfish aristocrats' Gladstone called them.

When Hugh spoke to the House again on this issue Gladstone was more generous to the wayward Whig:

> *I have no words to express my sorrow for the deeply important step you are taking; but ... as far as the tone and temper of your speech were concerned, I heard it with the utmost pleasure and thought it more than sustained your reputation for all the high qualities which have given you so high a place in the affection of your friends and in the public esteem.*

Defeated on this issue, the Cabinet resigned. Gladstone held that Grosvenor had 'taken the chief part' in destroying the 1866 Reform Bill, but Hugh wanted change and supported the Tory Disraeli's Reform Bill. Despite this, in 1874 Gladstone recommended Hugh for a dukedom. Chester Cathedral bells rang out and its mayor and corporation proceeded 'in state' to Eaton to present an address praising

> *... the faithful services rendered by Your Grace during the many years you ably represented your seat in Parliament; the active and generous aid you have always extended to all efforts to further the good and*

Katherine, second wife of the First Duke, by Sir John Everett Millais.

general welfare; the munificence of your charity; and above all your upright honourable and useful life.

The Duke interested himself in social legislation that might help the poor and in 1878 he seconded a bill to open public museums and art galleries on Sunday afternoons. It failed, but he allowed public access at those hours to the Grosvenor House picture-gallery.

Hugh held a coming of age party at Eaton for his son Victor and there was a week of feasting, fireworks and dancing. Five thousand were entertained in the grounds, while bands and the Yeomanry marched to Chester before the family's carriage through cheering crowds. Victor's wife-to-be, 19-year-old Lady Sibell Lumley, was with him. The youngest daughter of the Earl of Scarborough, she was passionate and ethereal.

To Victor and Sibell at Saighton Grange near Eaton Constance (Cuckoo), Lettice and Hugh (Bendor) were born but Victor suffered from

The First Duke of Westminster

epilepsy and, weakened by the condition, he shunned public life. His passion was engineering. The Times later recorded: 'He was frequently to be found in railway workshops at Crewe, and oftener still driving the "Wild Irishman" between London and Holyhead'. Observing him in 1880 his 84-four year old grandmother Elizabeth was shocked 'to find Victor a sad spectacle and quite altered from when I saw him eleven years ago – enormous, untidy and with a disagreeable underbred expression.' Victor died in his 31st year when his son Bendor was but four years old.

Meanwhile in 1875 Constance, aged 45, had contracted Bright's Disease. The Queen in the summer of 1880 visited her at Grosvenor House. On 19 December of that year the Queen at Osborne recorded: 'Had a telegram from the Duke of Westminster saying it was all over. Too sad.' The Prince of Wales and Mr Gladstone were amongst those who attended the burial at Eccleston.

Two years later the 58-year-old Duke married again. His bride was Katherine, aged 24, sister of his daughter-in-law and daughter of Lord Chesham at whose funeral but a month earlier they had met. Katie, as she was known, charmed stepchildren older than her and bore the Duke four children. Eaton became a convivial house for parties, theatricals and games. Great house parties gathered and the royal family visited. Hugh's ten-year-old granddaughter wrote in her diary:

> After ten we all went to the Big House to see people and the Prince of Wales who asked Mama what our names were. We saw Prince Eddy and Prince George and Prince George gave me a ride in the Bath chair down the passage. He was very nice.

The turf engaged the Duke's interest. By the purchase of Doncaster in

OPPOSITE UPPER:
Wrexham Road Farm, Eccleston, designed by John Douglas.

OPPOSITE LOWER:
The Gardener's bothy at Eccleston, designed by John Douglas

The 1880 Derby. *Bend Or*, ridden by Fred Archer, coming from behind to beat *Robert the Devil*.

FOR HIS GRACE THE DUKE OF WESTMINSTER K.G.

DOUGLAS & FORDHAM ARCHTS

LARDER

KITCHEN

LAVATORY   WC

HEATING CELL

PORCH   HALL   CORRIDOR

SITTING RM   MESS RM   BEDROOM

GROUND PLAN.

BATH RM   WC   BEDROOM

LINEN

2 BEDROOMS ON 2ND FLOOR   CORRIDOR

BEDROOM   BED RM   BED RM   BEDROOM

1ST FLOOR PLAN

1875 for the record sum of 14,000 guineas he re-established at Eaton a magnificent stud. In 1880 Fred Archer, wearing the Duke's 'yellow, black cap' colours, rode Bendor to victory in the Derby – the famed horse's name became the nickname of the Duke's grandson. Twice Hugh's horses won the Triple Crown. Another Derby winner, Ormonde, who never knew defeat, was guest at a garden party at Grosvenor House in 1886. Hugh's granddaughters Cuckoo and Lettice aged eleven and ten wrote:

> *Daddy and Katie called us to come to Grosvenor House as there is to be a grand party there and Ormonde is to be shown in the garden. When we got there most of the people had come. The first royal persons were the Prince and Princess of Wales and Prince and Princess William of Prussia. There was also the King of Denmark, the King and Queen of the Belgians, the King of Saxony, the Crown Prince of Portugal, the Duchess of Teck and her daughter, Prince Edward and Prince George, the Duke and Duchess of Mecklenburg-Strelitz, the Duke and Duchess of Edinburgh, Prince Ludwig of Bavaria, the Queen of Hawaii, the Crown Prince of Sweden and Norway and Prince Herman of Saxe-Weimar. There were also the Duke and Duchess of Sutherland, the Duke of Argyll, the Duke of Portland and Madame Albani, the great singer, and lots of other people. We enjoyed it so much. Ormonde was led round and round the garden, looking so beautiful and his coat shining in the sun. We all took a piece of his hair and longed to get on his back.*

The philanthropic enterprise run by Hugh from Grosvenor House and Eaton was as large as today's major charities. The Duke had concern for health, animal welfare, public access to land, and sobriety. He was President of five London hospitals, Chairman of the Queen's Jubilee Nursing Fund which provided district nurses for the sick poor and through which he was associated with Florence Nightingale, and Chairman of the Hampstead Heath Protection Society which had been founded at a meeting he convened at Grosvenor House at which Octavia Hill spoke. He pioneered cremation and headed an appeal for funds to enlarge Woking Crematorium, where his own body was to be burned. *The Times* observed of the Duke that he 'could pass from a race-course to a missionary meeting without incurring the censure of even the strictest.'

As a generous landlord he gave sites in London, Cheshire and North Wales for churches, rectories and schools, and oversaw the building of Queen Anne style houses throughout Mayfair. In Cheshire the Duke engaged the Arts and Crafts architect John Douglas amongst others to build 48 new farmhouses, 360 cottages, 11 lodges, 8 schools and 7 village halls as well as new churches at Pulford and Handbridge. For a new church at Eccleston, he commissioned GF Bodley.

In the 1880s the Duke opposed Gladstone's plan to grant Home Rule to the Irish; he saw the Irish leaders as 'miserable men whose bloody hands had brought ruin and murder to their country.' The matter strained relations between Hugh and Gladstone and Hugh sold Millais' portrait of Gladstone that had hung at Eaton. However, on Gladstone's birthday he sent flowers to Hawarden with this message:

Although I regret that I cannot follow you in the matter of Irish politics, I felt I may as a neighbour and friend, offer all congratulations today and send every wish for continued health and strength for many years to come.

Hugh and Gladstone were reconciled ten years later when they shared indignation over Turkish atrocities against the Armenians. When Gladstone died Hugh served as Chairman of his memorial committee.

In December 1899 the Duke himself died, aged 76. In that year he had successfully moved the second reading of the Seats for Shop Assistants Bill – 'a step in the direction of the prevention of cruelty to women'; he had stalked a fine stag in Scotland; he had shot 65 snipe in one and a half hours in Aldford, and attended his granddaughter Cuckoo's wedding from Grosvenor House. His ashes were buried in Eccleston. The Duke had wished no flowers, but the Queen insisted. A wreath of immortelles was placed on the coffin with the words: 'A mark of sincere respect and regard and esteem from Victoria R.I.'

George Wyndham, who had married Sibell, the Duke's widowed daughter-in-law, described the Duke in a private letter as 'the kindest man I ever knew'. To his own mother Wyndham wrote: 'We won't forget he remained young all his life and used his youth to make life happy for all about him.'

Bendor's step-father, The Rt Hon. George Wyndham

The First Duke of Westminster

10 'Bendor' – Hugh Grosvenor, Second Duke of Westminster (1879–1953)

Bendor's mother, Sibell, was adored by the brilliant young George Curzon, later Viceroy of India. But then her brother calculated that, widowed by Victor's death, 'eighty men were in love with her, including the curates, for she was of a religious disposition'. In 1887 she married George Wyndham, a 24-year-old Guards officer 'endowed,' as Curzon wryly remarked 'with the chivalry of a knight-errant, the fancy of the poet and the deep tenderness of a woman.' To Bendor, Wyndham was like an older brother; only eighteen years separated them. Wyndham had shared in the sparkling conversation of the circle of Oscar Wilde. Later, he brought Sibell into the company of the Souls, a coterie of enchanting women and their brilliant partners.

At Saighton, where George lived with Sibell and her children, there was little discipline, much affection. George described an energetic day:

Everyone was in the best of spirits at breakfast; Sibell complained that her egg had got a little cold and I said mine had got a little cough. In the morning we had athletic sports, high jump, long jump, and the jump hand in hand over hedges, then swinging till luncheon. In the afternoon cricket … then races … then fireworks.

Bendor flourished at Eton then joined the Royal Horse Guards. Urged by Wyndham, who had visited South Africa, Bendor accepted a posting in Cape Town as aide-de-camp to Sir Alfred Milner, the Governor General. He observed the Bloemfontein Conference between Paul Kruger and Sir Alfred. When hostilities began Bendor became ADC to Field Marshal Lord Roberts from whom he learned that rapid mobility of troops was of great tactical importance. He thrived on the excitement of war. With the young Winston Churchill he was ambushed in a train by mounted Afrikaaners, which shared danger sealed their lifelong friendship. Later Bendor was in the front line at Bergandal Kopje, a hard-fought tussle. When he returned to Cheshire at the war's end as the new Duke he received a hero's welcome.

Bendor's income was now unparalleled in England – 'a guinea a minute'. He married a childhood friend, Constance Cornwallis-West of Ruthin Castle, known as Shelagh, whose mother Patsy had been a famous beauty favoured by the Prince of Wales. An excellent horsewoman, Shelagh loved gardening, could cast a fly and was a self-assured hostess. Ursula was born in 1902 and an heir, Edward, in 1904.

King Edward was entertained at Eaton, as were the Prince and Princess of Wales, and Churchill, Milner and Roberts. King Alfonso of Spain visited

Lady Sibell Grosvenor, mother of Bendor, later Second Duke.

for polo matches. Cricket and tennis weeks were established and winter shooting parties too. George Wyndham observed of the changes Bendor had made:

> *The whole place has been turned into the embodiment of a boy's holi-*
> *day ... He has constructed a steeple-chase course and a mile-and-a-half*
> *of high tarred rails ... The stables are crammed with hunters,*
> *chase-horses, polo-ponies, Basutos, carriage-horses, American trotters*
> *and two motor cars. But it's all very boyish and delightful: no luxury.*

Bendor rode in the Grand National in 1904 but fell painfully and his horse had to be shot. He turned from competitive riding. For salmon fishing Shelagh and he stayed at Lochmore, in Scotland. Bendor developed a passion for car and speedboat racing and in 'Ursula' won the Coupe de Nations in Monte Carlo in 1909 and 1910.

He became President of the Imperial South African Association which

Bendor on his return from the Boer War.

39

Wyndham chaired. Milner later said the Duke was one who had taken 'an unobtrusive but most important part in repairing the ravages of war, who has supplemented by his private liberality immense public efforts made for its recuperation.' He acquired 30,000 acres of land near Bloemfontein. Sixteen model farms were designed and young Cheshire farmers sent as tenants were able gradually to buy their properties. Bendor liked to visit this idealistic project until recurrent tropical fevers kept him away.

The year 1909 was tumultuous for Bendor. The threat to inherited wealth in Lloyd George's budget unsettled him. He determined to sell the Halkyn estate and invest overseas. Then his dear son Edward died after appendix surgery at Eaton. The delay in calling a surgeon provoked family recriminations. Meanwhile the Cornwallis-Wests sought financial aid on a scale to irritate. Bendor palled at the artificiality of the social round. From Shelagh who loved it he became estranged. Bendor and Shelagh entertained together at a supper party in Grosvenor House in 1911 which gathered among others 27 princes and the Austrian Archduke. But it was a swan song, just as the European harmony that it expressed would disintegrate in the Great War's slaughter.

Wilfred Scawen Blunt wrote of Bendor at this time:

He is a kind, good-humoured fellow, like a great Newfoundland puppy, much given to riotous amusements and sports, with horses, motors and ladies. The fast life clearly suits him, for he looks the model of health and strength.

Bendor's ladies were typically talented and self-made. He liaised with Gertie Miller, a Bradford girl famed as a musical-comedy star and elegant dancer, with Anna Pavlova, the ballerina, and with Coco Chanel, the couturière. Courtly people observed with disapproval his move from aristocratic society towards that of the theatre and Café.

War, as was its wont, energized Bendor. In 1914 he went to the Front taking his Rolls Royce and chauffeur, George Powell. Appalled at the

Constance, Duchess of Westminster (known as Shelagh), Bendor's first wife, by Sir Frank Dicksee.

Bendor in an armoured car of his squadron in the First World War.

The handwritten guest list (left side):

SUPPER   GROSVENOR HOUSE   MONDAY   26 JUNE 1911

H.I.H Crown Prince of Germany
The Duke of Westminster
H.I.H. Hereditary Prince Youssouf Effendi of Turkey
H.I.H. Arch Duke Karl Franz of Austria
H.I.H. Grand Duke Boris of Russia
H.R.H Infante Don Fernando of Spain
H.I.H. Prince Higashi-Fushimi of Japan
H.R.H Crown Prince of Greece
H.R.H. Crown Prince of Roumania
H.R.H Prince Alexander of Servia
H.R.H Crown Prince of Denmark
H.R.H. Crown Prince of Sweden
H.R.H Crown Prince of Bulgaria
H.R.H Prince Danilo of Montenegro
H.R.H Prince Chakrabhongs of Pitsanulok
H.R.H Grand Duke of Hesse
H.R.H. Grand Duke of Mecklenburg Schwerin
Mr John Hayes Hammond
Vice Admiral Jacques de Jonquières
H.R.H Duke of Connaught
His Ex The French Ambassador
His Ex The Russian Ambassador
His Ex The Austrian Ambassador
His Ex The United States Ambassador
His Ex The Spanish Ambassador
His Ex The Japanese Ambassador
H.R.H Prince Henry of Prussia
H.R.H Duke Albrecht of Wurtemburg
H.R.H Prince Rupert of Bavaria
H.R.H Prince John George of Saxony
H.R.H Prince Henry of the Netherlands

The Duchess of Westminster
H.I.H Crown Princess of Germany
H.I.H Princess Higashi Fushimi of Japan
H.R.H Crown Princess of Greece
H.R.H. Crown Princess of Roumania
H.R.H Crown Princess of Sweden
H.R.H Princess Militza of Montenegro
H.R.H Grand Duchess of Hesse
H.R.H Grand Duchess of Mecklenburg Schwerin
H.R.H Princess Patricia of Connaught
H.R.H Duchess of Coburg
H.R.H Princess Henry of Battenberg
Mrs J Hayes Hammond
H.R.H Duchess of Connaught
Duchess of Rutland
H.R.H Princess Alexander of Teck
Countess Benckendorff
Mrs Whitelaw Reid
Madame de Villa Urrutia
Madame Kato
Countess Torby
H.R.H Princess of Saxe-Meiningen
H.R.H. Princess Fred'k Charles of Hesse
H.R.H Princess John George of Saxony
H.R.H Princess George of Greece
H.R.H Princess Maximilian of Baden
Marchioness of Winchester
Marchioness of Graham
H.H. The Duchess of Teck
Duchess of Santona
H.H. The Newab Sultan Begam of Bhopal
· See over

Reception at Grosvenor House, June 1911. Guest list, first page.

stalemate of the trenches, he mused upon military mobility. Returning home he gave cars from his garages for experimental work and urged on Churchill the adoption of armoured vehicles. He formed and largely financed a squadron of armoured cars which saw action in France, then went to Egypt where its tactical value was proved in the dash to Bir Hakkim to rescue 91 English prisoners of war. Bendor was recommended for a VC. Sir John Maxwell wrote of him:

A less determined or resourceful commander might well have shirked the responsibility of taking cars on the first occasion 30 miles, and on the second 115 miles, into unknown desert with the uncertainty of the cars being

Bendor in 1924, by Sir William Orpen.

The Second Duke of Westminster

able to negotiate the country and the amount of resistance that was likely to be encountered. I venture to think these actions constitute a record in the History of War.

In the event Bendor received the DSO. After leaving North Africa due to fever he became Churchill's personal assistant at the Ministry of Munitions and accompanied Churchill to Paris to meet Foch and Clemenceau.

Bendor divorced Shelagh in 1919 and married the 29-year-old Violet Rowley the following year. That marriage lasted only until 1926. Grosvenor House was sold and Bendor parted with many of its pictures. Detmar Blow, the surveyor to the Grosvenor estate, had adapted a design of Sir Herbert Baker's to provide for the Duke a hunting lodge in Mimizan on Les Landes, south of Bordeaux. There, Bendor relaxed in the company of real friends. Winston Churchill liked to paint at Mimizan. Hounds and horses for the stables were transported from England, and wild boar were chased. Often Bendor was restless; he sped between Lochmore and Mimizan, Monte Carlo and Biarritz on the 'Flying Cloud', a four masted schooner, or the 'Cutty Sark', a luxurious steam-powered former destroyer.

In 1929, while dining with Lord Beaverbrook in the Café de Paris in London, he met Loelia Ponsonby. She recorded:

I was immediately struck by his good looks and 'presence'. The Duke of Westminster! But how can I explain what he represented? He stood for dash, glamour and fast living. I did not really know anything definite about him, but I had a vague idea that he was immensely rich, owned great slabs of Mayfair and Belgravia, and shot, hunted, played polo, cruised about the world on a yacht, had been married twice, and was a legend, almost a myth.

Bendor with Mlle Coco Chanel at the Grand National, 1925.

LEFT:
Loelia Ponsonby, Bendor's third wife.

FAR LEFT:
Loelia, trailing behind the Duke.

They married in 1930. Loelia arriving at Eaton with its myriad servants observed, 'It's not a house; it's a town'. They lived together for five years.

Hilaire Belloc, the poet, was welcomed at Eaton. Bendor like Belloc travelled to the political right. Wealth, the Duke believed, was endangered by Communism. He joined The Link, a society which admired continental fascism. Once war broke out, however, Bendor reverted to being utterly and generously patriotic. The Cutty Sark he gave to the government to be again a destroyer. He loaned Eaton Hall which served first as a hospital for officers and then as the home of Dartmouth Naval College. Nor had Bendor's friendship with Churchill been severed. James Stuart wrote thus of Churchill:

> *[Winston] had a great friend in the late Duke of Westminster with whom he used to dine quite often, even in the war when he seldom went out for a meal at all. 'Bendor,' he said, 'is one of my oldest friends. If he had not been a Duke he would have got the VC in the First War. He is incapable of expressing himself, but he is always thinking a hundred years ahead.'*

In 1947 Bendor divorced Loelia and married Anne (Nancy) Sullivan from County Cork. 'I had to wait seventy years to find happiness,' he often said. He mellowed; even his anxiety at having no direct heir dissipated. Kind Nancy was knowledgeable about racing. By charm and cheerful adap-

Anne (Nancy), Bendor's fourth wife, wearing the Westminster tiara for the Queen's Coronation, 1953.

43

tation to his impulsive plans she brought out the best in him. Mimizan had burned down in 1947, but Nancy loved Lochmore and Eaton and the people there and, with Bendor, received the loyalty and affection of their large staff.

Guided by his agent, George Ridley, Bendor invested abroad and diversified. A sheep station was bought in Wagga Wagga, office blocks in Melbourne, development land in Canada including Annacis Island in the Frazer River, and eight thousand acres in Norfolk. Ridley drew up a will that the Duke signed in November 1952. It ensured that the bulk of Bendor's fortune, estimated at over 50 million pounds, would in due course devolve upon the infant who did become the sixth Duke. Even so on Bendor's death in 1953 £19,000,000 was paid in death duties, a record for the Revenue. To help meet the bill the Rubens' The Adoration of the Magi, now in King's College Chapel, Cambridge, was sold.

Bendor died at Lochmore on returning with Nancy from a fishing expedition by yacht to Norway. 'I've never been so happy in my life,' he had declared. The diarist Chips Channon captured his essence:

So Bend Or, the great Duke of Westminster, is dead at last; magnificent, courteous, a mixture of Henry the Eighth and Lorenzo il Magnifico, he lived for pleasure – and women – for seventy-four years. He wealth was incalculable; his charm overwhelming; but he was restless, spoilt, irritable, and rather splendid in a very English way.

Anne, Duchess of Westminster leading her steeple-chaser Arkle, winner of the Cheltenham Gold Cup in 1964, 1965 and 1966.

II William Grosvenor, Third Duke (1894–1963); Gerald Grosvenor, Fourth Duke (1907–1967); Robert Grosvenor, Fifth Duke (1910–1979)

Gerald Grosvenor, Fourth Duke
of Westminster.

William was surprised to become Duke. It had been expected that Capt. Robert Grosvenor, Bendor's first cousin would inherit, but he had died just five weeks before Bendor, and Robert's only son Hugh, a Second Lieutenant, had been killed six years earlier during armoured-car exercises in Berkshire.

William's father, Henry, son of the first Duke, had married Mina Erskine-Wemyss who, having given birth to two daughters, died in 1894 the day after being delivered of William. Queen Victoria had written Henry a message of sympathy in which she expressed some gratification 'that the poor little boy whose birth cost his poor mother her life is thriving.' But William thrived little. He remained simple, too frail to attend school. Throughout his life he was cared for, living in his adult years on a smallholding in Sussex. 'All I wish,' he said, 'is to be left alone in peace to breed my ducks. As far as I can tell, I intend to remain here in Whitstable.'

Financial and administrative responsibility was enjoyed by George Ridley who, relatively unbridled, was able to encourage new Grosvenor ventures both abroad and in Britain. Duke William neither visited Eaton nor occupied his seat in the Lords.

Eaton Hall was used as an army officers' training school. By 1960 the building was somewhat ragged from 20 years' military occupation, so in 1963 it was demolished, the chapel, clock tower and stables alone remaining. The age of the house-parties had ended.

On Duke William's death the succession passed to Gerald; his father Lord Hugh Grosvenor, son of the first Duke and of his second wife, Katie, had been killed, aged 30, at Ypres in 1914. Brought up in County Fermanagh, Gerald attended Eton and Sandhurst and joined the 9th Lancers in 1926. He served in North Africa in the war of 1939–45, being raised to the rank of Lieutenant Colonel and awarded the DSO. Soon after the D. Day landings he was wounded by shrapnel. The leg wound troubled him in later life, in fact a court ruled that his death over twenty years later was caused by it, as a consequence of which death duties were not levied on his estate.

Gerald and Sally, his wife, lived at Saighton Grange. The Duke's natural humility was admired in the region and the former soldier flourished as farmer and sportsman. He exhibited his own Dairy Shorthorn cattle, enjoyed the shoot on the Eaton estate, and served as Honorary Colonel of the Cheshire Yeomanry. He was President of the Royal Society of St George through which he sought to promote amongst the English a greater interest in their patron saint. Being without children and not very fit during his four years as Duke, Gerald collaborated in estate matters with Robert, his brother and heir.

Robert succeeded in 1967. As a young man he had been a keen sailor, competing in several Fastnet races in the 1930s. He pursued a short career in the City before the outbreak of war. Having enlisted in the Royal Artillery, he, like his brother, rose to be a Colonel and served in the Desert and Palestine. He then joined Hennell and Co., silversmiths, of which he became managing director.

Viola Lyttelton, a concert pianist and daughter of the eighth Viscount Cobham, became his wife in 1946, and the family, with children Leonora, Gerald and Jane, made a home in Ely Lodge on an island in Loch Erne, County Fermanagh. Robert became Honorary Colonel of the North Irish

Robert Grosvenor, Fifth Duke of Westminster, formerly MP for Fermanagh and South Tyrone.

The Fifth Duke of Westminster and Earl Grosvenor, by Norman Hepple.

Gerald, Sixth Duke of Westminster, with his wife Natalia, Hugh and Viola.

Horse, a territorial regiment. In 1955 he was returned as Ulster Unionist Member of Parliament for Fermanagh and South Tyrone and from 1957 to 1959 served as Parliamentary Private Secretary to Selwyn Lloyd, the Foreign Secretary. For nine years he held his seat in Westminster, and subsequently was Senator for three years in Northern Ireland.

On assuming the Dukedom, Robert moved to Eaton. To build a new hall he engaged as architect John Dennys, his wife Viola's brother-in-law. The house, built in two and a half years, was white, flat roofed, uncompromisingly modern, and delightful within. It gleamed like a liner.

Robert, keenly interested in the progress of the now world-wide Grosvenor Estate, travelled to Canada and Australia. He also set up the

The Later Dukes of Westminster

Maritime Trust at the behest of Prince Philip, thus resuming his nautical interest. In 1977 he was appointed Lord Lieutenant of Fermanagh, and it was in Northern Ireland at Ely Lodge that he died after a long illness. His son, the twenty-seven year old Gerald, succeeded him, to become the 6th Duke of Westminster.

Virtus non stemma – 'virtue not lineage' – is the Grosvenor's ancient motto. This is paradoxical in a family eminent in Cheshire for a millennium. Yet rarely have Grosvenors rested on their laurels. This history has shown that the demands of good landlordship and concern for the community have repeatedly driven family members, past and present, to the energetic practice of public 'virtue'.

His Grace, Gerald, Duke of
Westminster.